Prayer in All Things

A Saint Benedict's · Saint John's
Prayer Book

Kate E. Ritger
Michael Kwatera, O.S.B.
Editors

LITURGICAL PRESS
Collegeville, Minnesota

www.litpress.org

1   2   3   4   5   6   7   8

Library of Congress Cataloging-in-Publication Data

Prayer in all things : a Saint Benedict's, Saint John's prayer
    book / [edited by] Kate E. Ritger, Michael Kwatera.
        p.   cm.
    Includes bibliographical references.
    ISBN 0-8146-2981-4 (pbk. : alk. paper)
    1. Catholic Church—Prayer-books and devotions—
English.   I. Ritger, Kate E., 1981–   II. Kwatera, Michael.

BX2130.P74 2004
242'.802—dc22

                                                              2003026344

Contents

Preface

"Listen carefully, my child, to my instructions, and attend to them with the ear of your heart."[1]

I was drawn to Saint Benedict's and Saint John's five years ago by the schools' three thousand plus acres, strong academics (particularly in theology and education—my fields of study), Catholic community, and Benedictine hospitality, epitomized by that scrumptious loaf of Bennie or Johnnie bread! I believe Benedictine hospitality is the journey to listen with the ear of one's heart to the Spirit of God in ourselves, others, and the earth. Hospitality and prayerful listening surround us in this space we call "St. Ben's" and "St. John's."

I have found the Liturgy of the Hours to be an example of these Benedictine values. I was drawn to the Liturgy of the Hours at Saint John's by an emptiness I experienced inside myself, an emptiness dug by relational self-doubt and personal inadequacy. The Liturgy of the Hours provided a much-needed haven for me to sit with God and myself, and it was during this prayer time that I could breathe and begin to listen to God working in my life. As the demands of school amplified and my relational turmoil remained, my gratitude for the respectful silence at the Liturgy of the Hours grew. It was there, in the midst of communal prayer and deep listening, that this prayer book was introduced to me.

Before you is a prayer book and a commitment to Benedictine hospitality and listening. It is our intention to bring together the prayers of our communities—diverse, humble, and searching. No matter who you are, there are prayers here to connect us to each other. Some prayers in this book have only one line and reside in us throughout the day. Other prayers could take years to pray through but that is part of the journey of growing in Benedictine hospitality and listening. Blessings on this journey together.

I wish to thank all who submitted prayers and photos to this project. It has been a great blessing to share the prayers of your hearts. I would also like to thank Cyril Gorman, O.S.B., for "singing my praises" and inviting me to the project in the first place. Finally, thank you to Michael Kwatera, O.S.B., for challenging and affirming me, and remaining committed to our work together.

Peace,
Kate E. Ritger

Introduction

Dutch poet Simon Vinkenoog has said that "prayer is coming to share a greater inward space."[2] God's Holy Spirit, the source of all our prayer, opens the door to that "inner room" where Jesus bids us pray (Matt 6:6; NAB). And there, in the inner chamber of our hearts, we meet God, but also other people: those we pray with, those we pray for, and those who pray for us.

The prayers in this collection have been composed or suggested by people who have shared the inside spaces and outdoor areas of two central Minnesota campuses: Saint Benedict's (Monastery and College) in Saint Joseph and Saint John's (Abbey, University, Preparatory School—and Liturgical Press) in Collegeville. Here the witness of monastic women and men, and of those who share Benedictine values as teachers and students, administrators and staff members, alumni and alumnae, oblates and friends, gives a human face to the Benedictine motto: "Prayer and Work." Through their own compositions or borrowings from others, these prayerful people invite you to share a greater inward space with them.

This is very much a "pick and choose" book. There are prayers for times of day, occasions of need, periods of activity, and moments of rest. There are verbal and visual stepping stones to prayer and reflection, depending on how the Spirit whets your appetite. The texts are as different as the people who offered them. What is most desirable is that these prayers help those who pray them to become living words of praise, petition, repentance, and thanksgiving. For, to paraphrase Saint Augustine, a Christian should be a prayer from head to foot.

My special thanks go to Kate E. Ritger, coeditor of this book, for her patience and diligence as we shaped its form and content. Together we express abundant thanks to the members of the board that reviewed the manuscript and gave helpful suggestions for its improvement: Mara Faulkner, O.S.B.; Thomas Jones; Robert Pierson, O.S.B.; and Theresa Schumacher, O.S.B.

Lastly, I wish to gratefully acknowledge Brother Frank Kacmarcik, Obl.S.B. (✠February 22, 2004). This prayer book, the last one he worked on during his long career as a teacher of the Word in art, reflects his passionate concern for quality and excellence in everything we use to worship God.

Michael Kwatera, O.S.B.

Peace to All Who Enter Here

Let us be grateful
    to the men and women
    who
    century after century
    have enriched
        challenged
        entertained
    humankind
    by written words.
    Let us be grateful, too,
    to all who
    in whatever way
    have preserved them
    so that
    in the Providence of God
    ever present
    we may wisely build
    the future
    on the past.

M. Linnea Welter, O.S.B.

I

[Jesus said:]
"Ask, and it will be given to you;
search, and you will find;
knock, and the door will be opened for you.
For everyone who asks receives,
and everyone who searches finds,
and for everyone who knocks,
the door will be opened . . .
If you then, who are evil,
know how to give good gifts to your children,
how much more will your Father in heaven
give good things to those who ask him!"

(Matt 7:7-8, 11)

God, come to my assistance.

Psalm 70:1—the traditional way of beginning some of the prayers of the Liturgy of the Hours.[3]

Collect from an Office of Saint Benedict

Raise up in your Church, O Lord,
the spirit that animated
    our Holy Father Benedict;
that, filled with the same spirit,
we may strive to love what he loved,
and practice what he taught.
We ask this through Christ our Lord.
    Amen.[4]

Prayer for Families

O Lord Jesus,
you are the center of our family.
You humbled yourself
        and came to live among us.
The greater part of your life
was spent in your home
        with Joseph and Mary.
Be with our family.
Let your peace be with us!
Help us to do your will
in all that we say or do.
Guide us, Jesus, in our family decisions,
in our financial needs and worries,
in our work, our play, and our study.
Give us a strong faith;
strengthen our relationship with you.
O Lord, keep us on the path to the Father!
We ask this in your holy name. Amen.[5]

Prayer for the Benedictine Communities
of Saint John's Abbey
and Saint Benedict's Monastery

Praise and thanksgiving to you,
God of teachers and learners,
for instructing your Church
through the holy Rule of Saint Benedict.
This humble father and guide of monks
and his sister, Saint Scholastica,
bid us prefer nothing to the love of Christ
as we run the way of God's commandments.

Send your blessing
upon the Benedictine monks of Saint John's
        Abbey
and upon the Sisters of Saint Benedict's
        Monastery.
Strengthen their zeal for glorifying you
        through
community life, liturgy and the arts,
education, and all their varied ministries,
so that, placing their hope in you alone,
they may joyfully advance together
on the way to their heavenly home.
We ask this through Christ our Lord. Amen.

Michael Kwatera, O.S.B.

Prayer for World Peace

Great God, who has told us
"Vengeance is mine,"
save us from ourselves
save us from the vengeance in our hearts
and the acid in our souls.

Save us from our desire to hurt
        as we have been hurt,
to punish as we have been punished,
to terrorize as we have been terrorized.

Give us the strength it takes
to listen rather than to judge,
to trust rather than to fear,
to try again and again
to make peace even when peace eludes us.
We ask, O God, for the grace
to be our best selves.
We ask for the vision
to be builders of the human community
rather than its destroyers.
We ask for the humility as a people
to understand the fears and hopes
        of other peoples.
We ask for the love it takes
to bequeath to the children
        of the world to come
more than the failures of our own making.

We ask for the heart it takes
to care for all the peoples
of Afghanistan and Iraq,
        of Palestine and Israel
as well as for ourselves.

Give us the depth of soul, O God,
to constrain our might,
to resist the temptations of power,
to refuse to attack the attackable,
to understand
that vengeance begets violence,
and to bring peace—not war—
        wherever we go.

For You, O God, have been merciful to us.
For You, O God, have been patient with us.
For You, O God, have been gracious to us.

And so may we be merciful
and patient
and gracious
and trusting
with these others whom you also love.

This we ask through Jesus,
the one without vengeance in his heart.
This we ask for ever and ever. Amen.

Joan D. Chittister, O.S.B.[6]

Prayer for Peace

Praise to you,
      Father of our Lord Jesus Christ,
for sending your only Son to be our Savior.
Through his death and resurrection,
he is the gift of your peace
for all times and peoples.
In his most sacred name,
we ask you to unite your Church
and to preserve it in the bonds of peace.
Guide our leaders
to work for harmony and peace
within our country
and among all nations of earth.
Bring conflicts to an end
and rescue the victims of human hatred.
Shield those who serve and protect us,
and preserve them from all harm.
Remove from our hearts
all that threatens peace
within our families and communities.

Fill us with zeal for justice and peace,
and deepen our respect for all human life.
Keep us in peace
and help us to be peacemakers
in our words and deeds.
We ask these blessings
through your Son, the Prince of Peace,
whose kingdom is with you
    and the Holy Spirit,
one God, for ever and ever. Amen.

Most Rev. John F. Kinney, Bishop of Saint Cloud[7]

A Prayer for Students and Teachers

Lord, you know the heart
        of each of us here.
You know what brings each of us
to this place of study and preparation
        for the future.
And you know what gifts, challenges,
        expectations, and problems
each of us brings here as well.
Look with compassionate eyes on us
whether we are weak or strong,
        doubtful or assured.
You know, Lord, that some among us
are burdened with worries
        about family members or friends,
finances, health,
        or struggles against addictions.
Give all of us what we need
to deal honestly with whatever challenges
        we have,
and let us help each other
        bear these sufferings.
Send all of us a great love for truth
wherever we may find it.
Give us, we pray,
        the words we need to speak,
and the open hearts we need
to listen attentively to each other.

In our explorations and research,
　　　may we see beyond the texts
to hear the echoes of your own truth
　　　and call,
and by your mysterious providence,
be prepared within
　　　to change the world about us,
including ourselves.
We ask your blessings
on all those who have made it possible
　　　for us to be here,
parents, friends, benefactors,
because they often have more confidence
　　　in us
than we ourselves have.
Amen.

Helen Rolfson, O.S.F.

A Prayer for the Campuses
of Saint John's and Saint Ben's

Lord, let these beautiful campuses
be a place of blessing for all who come here.
So many people come,
perhaps unable even to express
            the longings of their hearts.
May they find love, acceptance, invitation to
            communion here,
knowing themselves held in honor
            and respect by this community.
May the love of Christ
lead them to the graces they most need.

O beautiful fields and forest,
            lakes and wetlands,
with your marvelous flora and fauna,
            praise God.
O birds, fish, forests, flowers,
praise God by your great variety of life.
O wonders of the architecture and art
            that surround us here,
shape our hearts by your beauty.
O classrooms, offices, residence halls,
            meeting places, bookstores,
            and workplaces,
call us to work together
in this great task of becoming more human.

O chapels and dining rooms,
be parallel sacramentals of the final banquet,
　　　a witness to hospitality,
and a place of coming together
　　　and molding of community.
O monasteries, prominent,
　　　yet nearly invisible,
shape us by your ideals in following Christ.
O libraries, full of records new and ancient
of the search for wisdom and love and truth,
sing to us of the human endeavor
　　　for knowledge
and of the joy of learning.
O cemeteries, last residence of parishioners
　　　and monastics,
equalizer of abbots and children,
sing to us of resurrection hope.
O all campus inhabitants, long-
　　　and short-term, praise the Lord.
Amen.

Helen Rolfson, O.S.F.

A Prayer for Teachers and Students

Lord Jesus,
You are the teacher of teachers.
Before you we are all learners.
As we delve into life's mysteries,
each day carries lessons for us.
The joy of exploration, however,
        is most often mixed
with discouragement, darkness,
        and the toil of very hard work.
Enlighten our minds. Open our hearts.
Temper our timidity.
        Attune us to your voice within.
Graciously give us the courage to continue
        until the end,
and the will to follow
        our deepest convictions with fidelity,
for you yourself are the way and the truth
        and the life.
Give us the blessing of your presence
        in our studies,
and the will to work together
with commitment to the glory of God
and the good of all the world.
Amen.

Helen Rolfson, O.S.F.

Before beginning, pause and listen to Jesus say . . . *"I was in prison and you visited me."*

(Matt 25:36)

Jesus,
Look with compassion on those in prison.
Heal the broken,
Soften the hard of heart,
Console the innocent,
and reveal your presence
to those who seek you.
Jesus,
heal their victims;
give your peace and perseverance
to their families;
impart the gifts of justice and mercy
to those who judge;
grant patience and wisdom
to those who guard;
and give your special grace
to those who minister in your name.
Amen.[8]

Prayer for Vocations

Praise to you, loving God,
for we are always in your hand.
You know us, and so we live.
You call us, and so we are your people.

Remember, Lord, your Church.
Guide it as it continues in our world
the saving work of Jesus, your Son.

Give us more priests and deacons,
religious sisters and brothers,
        and lay ministers,
who will powerfully proclaim the Gospel in
        word and deed.
Prepare them to be good
        and generous servants,
so that they may deepen your people's faith
        through their ministry.
Empower them to be a source
        of greater hope and love
in the Body of Christ.

All glory and honor be yours,
        Giver of all good gifts,
through Jesus Christ, our Lord. Amen.

Michael Kwatera, O.S.B.

Prayer before Ministering at Liturgy

Blessed are you, Lord God,
by your angels and saints
    in the throne room of heaven
and by your holy people gathered
    as the Church on earth.
I join with worshipers
    of all times and places
to praise your glory revealed in Christ Jesus
and to give thanks for your saving deeds.
Send your Holy Spirit,
    source of all our prayer,
to all who serve your people at the liturgy.
Help us worship you in spirit and in truth.
Guide the thoughts of our hearts,
the words of our mouths,
    and the work of our hands,
so that our service may give you glory.
All honor and praise to you, loving Father,
through Jesus Christ, our Lord and brother,
in the power of the Holy Spirit,
both now and for ever. Amen.

Michael Kwatera, O.S.B.

Prayer to Jesus Christ

Christ the Savior, let all your disciples
find renewed strength in you.
Christ the peacemaker,
     let nations and peoples
embrace lasting reconciliation in you.
Christ the teacher, let students and teachers
savor abundant wisdom in you.
Christ the liberator, let those who suffer
     from sickness and poverty,
from injustice and prejudice,
     find speedy deliverance in you.
Christ the life-giver, let those who have died
put on everlasting glory in you.
Amen.

Michael Kwatera, O.S.B.

Song of Farewell

May the angels take you into Paradise;
may the martyrs come to welcome you
    on your way,
and lead you into the holy city Jerusalem.
May the choir of angels welcome you,
and with Lazarus who once was poor,
may you have everlasting rest.[9]

II

"Pray in the Spirit
at all times in every prayer
and supplication."

(Eph 6:18)

The Bottom Lands

As we walk beyond the field,
out into the tree laced lip of the marsh,
our feet begin to sink into the sodden land.

We separate to find our own easy path.

You have gone across the high grasses,
beyond these careful edges and out
into the midst of the marsh.

I still skirt the bog trees,
        stumble over exposed roots.
The trunks are dead,
Heavy branched but twigless,

stark against the single moon
and the leaves of the living trees.
I am gazing up, open mouthed,

Witness to my own subsumption.

In the middle, your feet are soaked
        through your socks.
The trees are wreathed around you,
the night sky gapes above you.

We call out.
        Our voices are muffled, half-heard.

I am saying to you now
that the way these fireflies light up
one after the other,
        and a thousand at the same time,

makes them a living set of stars
gathering around one white and blue moon
which I cannot even see.

Ryan Kutter

Lord, take me by the hand
  and walk with me. Amen.

Kate E. Ritger

Teach Me to Listen

Teach me to listen, O God,
to those nearest me,
my family, my friends, my co-workers.
Help me to be aware that
no matter what words I hear,
the message is,
"Accept the person I am. Listen to me."

Teach me to listen, my caring God,
to those far from me—
the whisper of the hopeless,
the plea of the forgotten,
the cry of the anguished.
Teach me to listen, O God my Mother,
to myself.
Help me to be less afraid
to trust the voice inside—
in the deepest part of me.
Teach me to listen, Holy Spirit,
for your voice—
in busyness and boredom,
        in certainty and in doubt,
in noise and in silence.

Teach me, Lord, to listen. Amen.

John Veltri, S.J.[10]

Prayer for the College of Saint Benedict
(based on its motto, *Sic luceat lux vestra,* "So
let your light shine" [see Matt 5:16])

O God, source of life and goodness,
your Holy Spirit gives us voice to cry out:
in every darkness, Christ our light!
in every weakness, Christ our might!
Brighten our lives with the radiance of the
    risen Christ:
like a blazing campfire dispelling night's
    terrors,
like the dancing flame presiding over the
    Olympics,
like a glowing altar candle spending itself in
    your service.
Scatter the darkness in every heart and in
    every place
with the light that comes from you
and is reflected in us.
Remove from us whatever can keep our
    light hidden:
pride and selfishness, fear and prejudice.
To you be praise, O God of eternal day,
through Jesus Christ, the sun that knows no
    setting,
in the power of the Spirit of truth,
for ever and ever. Amen.[11]

A Prayer to the Holy Spirit

O Holy Spirit of God,
        be our helper and guide.
Through our prayerful meditation
        on Scripture,
fill us with the spirit of wisdom
        and understanding,
the spirit of right judgment and courage,
the spirit of knowledge and reverence.
Pour out within us
the spirit of wonder and awe
        in your presence.
We ask this through Christ our Lord.
        Amen.[12]

The *Memorare*—a traditional Marian prayer

Remember, O most gracious Virgin Mary,
that never was it known
that anyone who fled to your protection,
implored your help
    or sought your intercession
was left unaided.
Inspired with this confidence,
I fly unto you, O Virgin of virgins,
    my mother.
To you I come; before you I stand,
    sinful and sorrowful.
O Mother of the Word Incarnate,
despise not my petitions, but in your mercy,
    hear and answer me.
Amen.[13]

Prayer to Mary

Mary, help me to become
    a woman like you,
so open to the will of God. Amen.

Verenice Ramler, O.S.B.

A Prayer before the Computer Screen
at the College of Saint Benedict •
Saint John's University

Lord,
our ethereal network that binds us
        all together
across this globe,
        and especially on our two campuses,
is a concrete reminder
of how interrelated we can be
        to one another.
May we use these instruments
        with great creativity,
a love of learning
        that links with desire for God,
with joy of discovery,
        and with moral discernment.
May the time we spend at work
        before the screen
be judiciously used;
may it not isolate us,
but help to join the hearts
        and minds of many
in seeking your truth, goodness, and beauty.

May we have patience with our own errors
          and searchings,
knowing that the "search function"
is a symbol of our own lives.
May your blessings be poured out
on those who remain available to assist us
in learning new things,
as well as on those
          who offer us technological assistance
          in our emergencies.
Amen.

Helen Rolfson, O.S.F.

Lord, for all those who need you
more than I . . . Amen.

Kate E. Ritger

Blessing a New Prayer Journal

Dear Lord,
Please bless this new journal,
and the time that I spend reflecting
     in its pages.
Bless me during my prayerful journeying
as I struggle and grow
and continue on my journey toward you.
Its pages are now empty;
     unblemished, white, unlived.
Where will I be when its pages are full
—full of love, pain,
     bursting with happy moments and
     tears
—where will I be?
Bless this journal
     and the time between its covers.
Amen.

Kate E. Ritger

My Lord!
We can do nothing without your help.
In the name of your divine compassion
do not let this soul be misled,
or turn aside from the path it has taken.
Give it your light,
to see that its well-being
depends on continuing along that path,
and to keep it well away
from the company of the wicked.

Saint Teresa of Avila[14]

Lord,
It is night.

The night is for stillness.
Let us be still in the presence of God.

It is night after a long day.
What has been done has been done;
what has not been done has not been done;
let it be.

The night is dark.
Let our fears of the darkness of the world
        and of our own lives
rest in you.

The night is quiet.
Let the quietness of your peace enfold us,
all dear to us,
and all who have no peace.

The night heralds the dawn.

Let us look expectantly to a new day,
new joys,
new possibilities.

In your name we pray.

Amen.[15]

III

"Do not worry about anything,
but in everything by prayer
and supplication with thanksgiving
let your requests be made known to God."

(Phil 4:6)

Serenity Prayer

God, grant me the serenity
      to accept the things I cannot change,
the courage to change the things I can,
and the wisdom to know the difference.

Prayer in Grief

God,
How can you let your people go?
How can they no longer live to praise you?
Is it within grief that we still love
and live with the one who is lost?
Are they closer now that they are gone?
Is the pain of their absence
        part of your being?
In our grief how do we know you?
We pray to know you. We hold faith in you.
Amen.

Edward Hackney

"Psalm 4"

I stretch out my arms for you, O Lord
For your glory I give my life

I'll drink of your cup as it is your will
For your people's salvation I give my life

You have given us all that is, O Lord
Through your gracious creating love
I give all that is back to you, O Lord
in grateful praise for your wondrous gifts

Let my will be yours to do your works
I give my soul for your peace and justice

I will be a fool to the world, O Lord
To do your will and return your love
In darkness they mock me
But in light you see the truth

Lord God, you are always with me
but I am seldom with you
I do not see your fingerprints
        on the leaves in autumn
or your spirit in the people I meet
Please open the eyes of my soul
so I can see your face
Let me feel your hand holding mine
in both this world and the next

Amen.

Steven Donatelle

Joshua Guimond, a Saint John's University student, has been missing since November 9, 2002, and has not been found up to this book's date of publication.

Josh: Roommate
Mock Trial co-captain
Politico
A young man
A bright future
My best friend
All these things you remain to me.

Josh, where are you?
Many long months have passed
　　　since we last saw you
Many months too long.
Every day we hope. Every day we pray.
We know you're out there. But where?

Lord, please help us
To keep the faith
To help each other
To love each other
To know that we need each other
To Keep Hope Alive.

Lord, please help us
To find our friend.

Wherever he is,
Watch over him
Guide him, like a shepherd, home again.

Josh, may God help you
To know our thoughts
To know we love you
To know we miss you
To know that our feelings
      cannot be expressed in words
To know that we will never stop searching
      until you come home.

Nick Hydukovich

Help me understand THY will not MY will.

Christian Breczinski

Prayer of Saint Francis

Lord, make me an instrument of your peace;
where there is hatred, let me sow love;
where there is injury, pardon;
where there is doubt, faith;
where there is despair, hope;
where there is darkness, light;
and where there is sadness, joy.

Grant that I may not so much seek
to be consoled as to console;
to be understood, as to understand;
to be loved as to love;
for it is in giving that we receive,
it is in pardoning that we are pardoned,
and it is in dying that we are born
       to eternal life.[16]

Prayer When Feeling Lonely

Lord, if I am to be alone,
let me remember
that it takes an isolated thread,
to wind itself around a tear
and mend a net.
All the other threads already have
their appointed places.

Lucie Johnson, Obl.S.B.

Lord, if your words be ours,
make them resonate within our hearts
awaken our ears
to the courage of your words
liberate us from the bondage of our fears
in-grown and home-grown
show us the light of your redeeming love
in our words, actions, and attitudes
Help us to care for one another.
Amen.

Nancy Gibbs, Obl.S.B.

To Christ of the Waves

These Waves
    Are for me
    A Tempest.
I shall perish, lost in an abysmal sea.
Yet,
    For You,
    Like that night in Galilee,
They are a lulling hush,
A Cradle of Respite, Relief
    From the labors of arduous love.
Exhaust me, impel me
    That I, too,
    in this sea,
        Might sleep.

Neville Ann Kelly

Father, I give these worries to you,
for they are worthless.
I know that you will be with me
through it all.
You will take care of all those things
that scare me. You will hold my heart,
and if I have the patience
       to leave it in your hands,
you will heal it and gently give it wings.
I love you, Abba.
Please make me into the person
you want me to be.
I am yours.
Amen.

Jennifer Wacek

The Universal Prayer

Lord, I believe in you: increase my faith.
I trust in you: strengthen my trust.
I love you: let me love you more and more.
I am sorry for my sins: deepen my sorrow.

I worship you as my first beginning,
I long for you as my last end,
I praise you as my constant helper,
and call on you as my loving protector.

Guide me by your wisdom,
correct me with your justice,
comfort me with your mercy,
protect me with your power.

I offer you, Lord, my thoughts:
        to be fixed on you;
my words: to have you for their theme;
my actions: to reflect my love for you;
my sufferings:
        to be endured for your greater glory.

I want to do what you ask of me:
in the way you ask,
for as long as you ask,
because you ask it.

Lord, enlighten my understanding,
strengthen my will,
purify my heart,
and make me holy.

Help me to repent of my past sins
and to resist temptation in the future.
Help me to rise above
        my human weaknesses
and to grow stronger as a Christian.

Let me love you, my Lord and my God,
and see myself as I really am:
a pilgrim in this world,
a Christian called to respect and love
all whose lives I touch,
those in authority over me
or those under my authority,
my friends and my enemies.

Help me to conquer anger with gentleness,
greed by generosity,
apathy by fervor.
Help me to forget myself
and reach out toward others.

Make me prudent in planning,
courageous in taking risks.
Make me patient in suffering,
        unassuming in prosperity.

Keep me, Lord, attentive at prayer,
temperate in food and drink,
diligent in my work,
firm in my good intentions.

Let my conscience be clear,
my conduct without fault,
my speech blameless,
my life well-ordered.

Put me on guard
        against my human weakness.
Let me cherish your love for me,
keep your law,
and come at last to your salvation.

Teach me to realize
        that this world is passing,
that my true future
        is the happiness of heaven,
that life on earth is short,
and the life to come eternal.

Help me to prepare for death
with a proper fear of judgment,
but a greater trust in your goodness.
Lead me safely through death
to the endless joy of heaven.

Grant this through Christ our Lord. Amen.

Attributed to Pope Clement XI[17]

Comfort and hold my weary body. Amen.

Kate E. Ritger

Prayer for Healing

Eternal Father,
Source of all mercy and love
out of love for us you sent your Son,
and willed that blood and water
flow from his side to cleanse us of sin
and restore lost innocence.
Hear the cry of each woman who mourns
the loss of her child to abortion.
Forgive her sin, restore her to your grace,
and still the terror of her heart
with a peace beyond all understanding.
Through the intercession
of the Blessed Virgin Mary,
Mother of all tenderness and our Mother,
strengthen her faith in you.
Give her the consolation to believe
that her child is now living in the Lord.
We ask this through Christ our Lord,
who conquered sin and death,
and who lives and reigns with you,
in the unity of the Holy Spirit,
one God, for ever and ever.
Amen.

Msgr. James Moroney[18]

An Adaptation of Psalm 131

No place for conceit before you,
No arrogant eyes.
I don't want to be busy with grand affairs,
Things I can't control anyway.
I want to be quiet,
Hushed like a child,
Resting on its mother's breast,
Resting in your love.

Vincent Smiles

Lord God, watch over me;
hold my hand as you embrace me.
Love me, surround me
        with your life giving presence.
Hold, embrace and love as you always do.
When I die I wish to be with you;
        always with you.
Along with all your saints I praise you,
that I may come to see your face,
with all your holy ones living and dead,
        in the next world.
Amen.

Steven Donatelle

IV

"Rejoice always,
pray without ceasing,
give thanks in all circumstances;
for this is the will of God
in Christ Jesus for you."

(1 Thess 5:16-18)

Waking to a New Day

Lord,
As I turn back the covers
and sit on the edge of the bed,
my eyes and mind still focusing,
thank you for bringing me
        safely through the night.
As I put my feet on the floor
let me remember
        the wondrous evolutionary process
that has been in place
        for thousands of years,
that makes this action possible.

What amazing creatures we are,
moving freely on two feet,
hands free to reach, to gesture, to touch,
to embrace, to hold, to be of service.
What enormous freedom comes to me
because of this pathway;
freedom to walk, to jump, to run, to dance,
to see far into the horizon.

Strengthen me, Lord,
to stand and walk in your love and grace.
Help me to embrace this day as gift,
as uniquely given for the first and last time.
Release in me the energy
for building up the community around me.
Amen.

John Klassen, O.S.B.,
Abbot of Saint John's Abbey

Teach Me the Songs of Your Truth

Teach me the songs of your truth, O Lord,
That I may bear fruit in you.
Open to me the music of your spirit,
That with every note I sing,
I may praise you.
Out of your kindness grant me this
For you are the answer to all our needs.
Alleluia!

David Haas[19]

In omnibus glorificetur Deus. = In all things
God may be glorified.
(1 Pet 4:11; *Rule of Saint Benedict,* 57:9)[20]
Source of the "IOGD" on the
Saint John's Quadrangle.

The Divine Praises

Blessed be God.
Blessed be His Holy Name.
Blessed be Jesus Christ,
    true God and true man.
Blessed be the name of Jesus.
Blessed be His Most Sacred Heart.
Blessed be His Most Precious Blood.
Blessed be Jesus
    in the Most Holy Sacrament of the altar.
Blessed be the Holy Spirit, the Paraclete.
Blessed be the great Mother of God,
    Mary most holy.
Blessed be her holy
    and Immaculate Conception.
Blessed be her glorious Assumption.
Blessed be the name of Mary,
    Virgin and Mother.
Blessed be Saint Joseph,
    her most chaste spouse.
Blessed be God
    in His angels and in His saints.[21]

Midmorning: Reflection on Psalm 1

The day has barely gotten underway, Lord,
and already I am scattered.
Already I've avoided a chore,
responded with a note of impatience,
sought to be noticed,
made an excuse,
daydreamed,
worried.
I am a tumbleweed
tossed about by the gusts of my whims.
Oh gather me!
Hold me in the stillness of your presence,
Write your name in my heart.
In the midst of the daily hubbub,
may I still remember you.
Help me trust you enough
        to root my life in your will,
to be quietly present
        to what you have given me to do.
Bless my work, Lord,
that out of these bumbling efforts
some good may come.

Lucie Johnson, Obl.S.B.

Help me to be more of my truest self . . .
more often. Amen.

Kate E. Ritger

Morning Prayer

In the songs of the morning
in blessings that rise
and in hope that takes root
in the midst of silence
gather us.

Meld
our slow steps and fast steps
our falterings and hesitations
our faithful walks
our repentance and return
and our simple waiting
into one path.

Through the voice of the young
and the words of the elder
through stories and prayers
and in quiet presence
come to us.

Through bread that is offered
and lives that are yielded,
through gifts to be shared,
and in our poverty
be with us.

With the little that we have
and the little that we are
send us.
May we dare to hope
that the crumbs of our trying
in your hands
will multiply.

Oh, take care of the people.
So many find themselves in isolated places
and they grow faint
looking for food.

Lucie Johnson, Obl.S.B.

Lord,
Thank you for this beautiful day!
Please help me to see the beauty
        in every day
and help others to see the beauty
        in your wonders.
Guide me through perils
        toward your brilliant light.
Amen.

Kate E. Ritger

May [God] support us all the day long,
till the shadows lengthen
    and the evening comes
and the busy world is hushed
and the fever of life is over
    and our work is done—
then in his mercy—
    may he give us a safe lodging
and a holy rest and peace at the last.
Amen.

Attributed to Cardinal John Henry Newman
(1801–1890)[22]

Night Prayer

"Even darkness is not dark to you;
the night is as bright as the day."

(Ps 139:12)

For your presence in the quiet
when all are gone
when armors crumble
and I'm only a child
who knows little
and can do even less
Thank you.
For listening to my heart
and hearing my thoughts
for carrying my doubts
for waiting with me
for being gentle
with my fears
Thank you.

For feeding me with your own life
for giving all you have
for walking in my shoes
all the way to the cross
for never turning away
no matter what the cost
Thank you.

For helping me to give
for inviting me to open
closed heart and grasping hands
for calling me to walk with you
for people to love
and for things to do
Thank you.

Lucie Johnson, Obl.S.B.

God of the horizon . . .
You showed the path
        to Abraham and to Sarah,
to Moses, and to Ruth.
I feel you are also showing me the path
        I am to follow.
Thank you for bringing me to this place.
As I gaze upon Lake Sagatagan,
and see your stars dancing on your lake
        in your moonlight,
I feel at peace.
I stand in awe before the beauty
        of your creation.
May this sense of peace that I feel tonight
always be part of who I am
and may this same peace be felt
        throughout the world.
I ask you this through your Son,
        Jesus Christ,
who lives and reigns with you
        in the unity of the Holy Spirit,
one God now and forever.

Amen.

Sherri Vallee

As I crawl into bed
Rest and rejuvenation . . . in you,
   O Mother. Amen.

Kate E. Ritger

On My Birthday

Heavenly Father,
Thank you for creating me
    and giving me another year of life.
Help me to use my talents
    to the best of my ability
so that my life is as fruitful
    as you have planned. Amen.

Kate E. Ritger

Gratitude

Before you, Lord,
    and before all your creation,
I come in gratitude.
All that I am, I receive from you.
I bow before you.
I touch the earth from which I came,
and make myself as small as I can.
I surrender to you all my ideas,
all I have done and left undone,
all my hopes and all my fears,
all my accomplishments
    and all my mistakes,
all I have and all I want.
Let me die to everything to which I cling
and receive life from your hands,
    day by day,
each hour a gift that opens before me.

Before those who have given me life,
physical and spiritual,
before parents and grandparents,
teachers and mentors,
ancestors to the beginning of time,
I bow in gratitude.
I know their love was always there,

Even when its expression was flawed
        or distorted
because of their own wounds.
Help me, Lord,
        to treasure their precious gift,
and to find ways to heal
        and repair in myself
that in which they were unskillful.
That I may love well,
bring joy to my children, and grandchildren,
to those whose lives I touch,
and so honor those who came before me.

Before those who are dear to my heart,
Those whom I love,
Those who love me,
I bow in gratitude.
Their love, Lord, has opened me to you,
helped me know goodness, brought me joy,
and nourished my life.
May their gift return to them
        a thousandfold.
May I nurture in my heart
        the attentiveness of their love
and be a blessing for others
as I have been blessed.

Before those who have hurt me
        and harmed me,
those who have made my life difficult,
those who have betrayed me,
those who hated and despised me,
those of whom I was afraid,
I bow in gratitude.
Their challenges have stretched me.
I have learned much
        about dark places within.
In time, compassion has taken root
        within me,
my heart has grown larger,
able to love and hold more.
Their gift seemed very bitter,
        but it was precious too.
Bless them, Lord,
and may the compassion they have fostered
envelop them also
and mend all their broken places.

Amen.

                                    Lucie Johnson, Obl.S.B.[23]

Prayer for College Alumni/ae

Loving God, we thank you for the men and
        women
who brightened our college years
and inspired us by their lives and works.
We pray that the ideals of Saint John's and
        Saint Benedict's
will be reflected in our lives and actions.
Let us illustrate in our lives
a sense of your presence, a welcome to others,
a willingness to listen to and respect those
        of different backgrounds,
a sense of stewardship for our earth
and a willingness to put the common good
before personal advantage.
Temper our work and activities
with the virtues of the Gospel,
with patience, love, generosity and
        compassion.
May the friendship, loyalty and laughter
we shared so joyously as students
continue to mark our personal relations.
May we use our talents and skills
for the good of our fellow human beings
and to advance the cause of peace and justice
in our so-often battered world.

May an awareness of our life and strength
        in Christ
help us through all the disappointments,
        failures and tragedies
that unavoidably mark human life.
May we share, along with our families,
friends, professors and mentors
an indomitable hope and even some serenity
in the face of war, illness and personal
        tragedy.
We make this prayer
through Jesus Christ, our Lord and brother.
        Amen.

Don Talafous, O.S.B.

Let nothing disturb you,
nothing alarm you:
while all things fade away
God is unchanging.
Be patient
And you will gain everything:
For with God in your heart
Nothing is lacking.
God meets your every need.

Saint Teresa of Avila[24]

Thanksgiving in the Spirit, for a Friend

*"The fruit of the Spirit is love, joy, peace,
patience, kindness, generosity, faithfulness,
gentleness, and self-control."*

(Gal 5:22-23)

Love

Nature-lover sees
Through bark and water's surface:
Supernatural, grace.

Joy

Travelers' resting place:
Her heart's spirit comfort gives,
Their own afire now.

Peace

When, when will it come?
Her heart seeks within, without:
Will we hear her now?

Patience

Her silence communes
With the people by her path:
Compassion her gift.

Kindness

In meadows and parks
Beauty surrounds her: the same
To her world is she.

Generosity

Glass, wick, wax, paper:
The map dims when the sun sets,
But the path does not.

Faithfulness

She to her dear ones,
As God has been to us: this
The essence of love.

Gentleness

Goods, fabric, food, Poor—
Hands touch: the artisan crafts
Her work. We are changed.

Self-Control

Discipline's freedom
Not on the musician lost:
She dances the same.

An S.J.U. alumnus[25]

V

"Devote yourselves to prayer,
keeping alert in it with thanksgiving."

(Col 4:2)

Prayer in Honor of Mother Benedicta Riepp,
American Foundress

Loving God, we praise and thank you
for the life and mission
    of Mother Benedicta Riepp.
Cherishing the privilege of her call,
and placing unconditional trust
    in your divine providence,
she dared to dream of a new era
for the vision and spirit of Benedict.
May her life of prayer and work inspire us
to move into our own uncharted future
with faith, hope, and love.
This we ask through Jesus, the Christ.
    Amen.

Ephrem Hollermann, O.S.B.,
Prioress of Saint Benedict's Monastery

"Psalm 1"

Lord, I wish to do your will
    it is out of grateful love.
Lord, it is you that I love.
Commandments you made
    for us to come near;
Commandments motivated
    by love.
To follow your word,
    the letter of your law
Is of little pleasure to you
    if it is not love
    that leads us
    to live your call.
In persecution I beg you,
    "Give patience and love to me."
I am near to you, Lord
    out of love, wonder and awe,
    draw me nearer to your mystery.
And those who injure,
        they are blind to your call.
Bless them and hold them
    gather them in,
Fill them and seal them with your love.

Steven Donatelle

"Psalm 2"

You are here God,
all around me.
But the eyes of my soul are blinded,
    by sin, confusion and restlessness.
In my heart it is you I trust
but the world draws me
        from my heart.

"Buy! Sell! Want! Need!"
shout the people all around me.
They tempt me for their own gain,
they call me aside from your path.

Wash clean these scabs
that cover my eyes.
Temper my will.
Temper my soul.
Not so I may be hard,
        harsh,
        and cruel
but that I may follow my heart
which leads me to you.

Grant me power
to turn down their greedy shouts,
so that my ears may hear
your call more clearly.

Aid me God,
for my heart is true!
But my will needs your help.
Your will no one can break,
your power can heal all things.
May my will be strengthened by you,
so that I may be strong
to follow my heart,
   which is living flesh of your will.

Steven Donatelle

Lord, Give us Words

Give us cheering words for the lonely,
Comforting words that bless . . .
Encouraging words for the hopeless,
Smiling words to bring happiness.
Give us patient words for the struggling,
Courteous words, so that rudeness ends,
Kind words for those who upset us . . .
Forgiving words for those who offend.
Give us faith-filled words that are positive,
That inspire optimism and zeal.
Teach us "the time to keep silence"
And the "time to speak" and to feel.
May we wait on You
         with prayerful thoughts,
For the wisdom You impart.
Give us acceptable words to express,
The meditations of our hearts.

Micky Meyer Mathewson[26]

Grant me open ears to listen to your word
in all of creation.

Christian Breczinski

A Writer's Daily Prayer

Mother Father God,
I thank you for this day and for the
Opportunity to praise you through
The talents you have given me.
I honor my mind and heart
As manifestations of your presence
On this earth—grant that my thoughts
And feelings be those of wholeness
        and healing for
Those with whom I come
In contact.
        I honor my senses as gifts from you—
Through their fullness I return to you—
        At every
Moment of the day—
Being fully cognizant of seeing
Hearing, smelling, touching, and
Tasting your Divine presence in myself
And those I love—I am truly blest.
As I embark upon my writing today
I call upon you—the Divine within—
My higher self to grant me joy and
Inspiration in the knowledge that
This day and every day is for
Your honor and glory.
Amen.

Kathleen O'Shea

Woven Together in Love

Lord,
    Weave our lives together in love
    Make us a patchwork of kindred souls
    Let the patterns of our lives
        come together as one
    Stitch together the brokenness
        and remnants of our past
to create a new design for living.

T. Todd Masman

The Caregiver

Two simple words. I care.

What more could I say or do?
 I have given all I have to give.
I have laughed with him.
Cried with him.
I have held him in my arms.
I have let him go.

How could I have thought this would be easy?
Where will I find the strength to go on?

Lord, I am tired.

Give me the strength
 to continue one more day.
Give me peace
 to calm the raging of my soul.
Give me patience when I am restless.
Give me love to share with my partner.
Give me hope
 to look for the promise of eternal life.

Amen.

T. Todd Masman

Maybe some day Lord,
there might be some one other than you
who will look at me
and see a beautiful, yet struggling
    reflection of your Son.
Maybe some one who would hold me
    tightly close,
even when I nervously
    and self-consciously shiver.
Some one who will share my prayers
and encourage me to share my hidden gifts.
Some day Lord. Maybe some day. Amen.

Kate E. Ritger

Lord, I praise You for Your omnipotence,
Your omniscience,
Your omnipresence,
Your boundless love, mercy,
      generosity and compassion.
You are the alpha and the omega.

Betty A. Sullivan Haas

Table Blessing

Loving God,
we ask you to bless this food
and to look kindly on those who have
        prepared it.
As we share this meal,
draw us closer to you and to each other
in the bond of love.
Show to all people,
especially those who lack enough to eat,
your goodness and loving-kindness.
To you, Sustainer of the needy,
be honor and glory through Jesus Christ,
both now and for ever. Amen.

Michael Kwatera, O.S.B.

Mary Stewart's Prayer

Keep us, O God, from all pettiness.
Let us be large in thought, in word, in deed.
Let us be done with fault-finding
      and leave off all self-seeking.
May we put away pretense
and meet each other face to face
without self-pity and without prejudice.
May we never be hasty in judgment,
      and always be generous.
Let us always take time for all things,
and make us to grow calm, serene,
      and gentle.
Teach us to put into action
      our better impulses,
to be straightforward and unafraid.
Grant that we may realize
that it is the little things in life
that create differences,
that, in the big things in life, we are one.
And, O Lord God,
      let us not forget to be kind.
Amen.[27]

The Jesus Prayer

Lord Jesus Christ, Son of God,
have mercy on me,
a sinner.

In Beauty We Walk—Navajo Night Chant

In beauty we walk.
With beauty before us we walk.
With beauty behind us we walk.
With beauty above us we walk.
With beauty above us and about us,
      we walk.
It is finished in beauty.[28]

Rosary

Wait here
and keep watch with me.

Blessed are you among women
and blessed is the fruit of your womb.

Blessed is he who listens
          to the children's cries
who takes on the pain and sin
          that strangles lives
and does not walk away.
Blessed is he who is afraid but does not run
who is alone and still trusts.

Mary.

As for me,
from the whisper of vulture wings
I have hid.
Abandoned my friend.
Sought to be spared from another's agony.
Said "I don't know him."
Oh just let me sleep
through babies dying
through mothers moaning
through spears and guns and screams
          and crosses burning.
I do not want to die.

Mother of God

See, he has fallen.
Oh why did he not fight back?
Why did he say
yes
yes
and yes again
to the blows and the jeers
to the rough lumber in the sun
while I avoided him
and lived a reasonable life
of measured compassion and safe altruism.
I lashed him with my fear
my gentility drove the nails.

Pray for us, sinners. Now

"It is finished"
So open and yielded on the cross
Emmanuel
all of all has been given away.

and in the hour of our death

There are no words left.

Lucie Johnson, Obl.S.B.

I love you, Mother.
I cling to you in this time of change
     in my life.
You will be my rock,
and I will trust in you.
You alone can understand
what I have been through
and where I am going.
I love you.
I follow you.
Amen.

Jennifer Wacek

VI

Jesus said: "If you abide in me, and my words abide in you, ask for whatever you wish and it will be done for you."

(John 15:7)

Prayer of a Prophet

"Do not say, 'I am only a boy';
for you shall go to all to whom I send you,
and you shall speak whatever I command you."

(Jer 1:7)

Lord, grant that I may hear Your commands
    and Your wise words.
Grant that I may find the words to speak
    Your truths,
And that I may have the strength of will
    to do as You wish.
For in as much as we are followers of Christ,
We are Your messengers
And we need Your strength and wisdom.
Amen.

Steven Donatelle

Put your words into my heart
      so that every breath from my mouth
      is in praise of you.

Christian Breczinski

"Psalm 3"

I come to you,
    tired and worn out.
    Worked-out, exhausted.
It is for you that I labor.
I come to you
    to know that my hands are building
        your church.
My hands that don't move brick
      or shape stone,
    hands that shape souls and move hearts.
I come to you empty,
    hoping that what I have poured out
    was from you.
    Hoping that you will fill me again
        so I can share
        more of your wonders.
I come to you for rest.
I come to you for wisdom.
I come to you to be sent out again.
I come to you so that others may come
        To you.
To you, Lord.
    To you.

Steven Donatelle

Dear Heavenly Comforter,
Help me to find what is missing;
missing in my life, missing in the Church,
missing from your people and their love.
"Do not be afraid, I am with you . . ."
    Amen.

Kate E. Ritger

Let us make our way together, Lord;
wherever you go
I must go:
and through whatever you pass,
there too I will pass.

Saint Teresa of Avila[29]

Lord,
Please help me to identify
    what is truly important in life.
Please guide my friends who are confused
about the way you are leading them.
Open them (and me!)
    to your love and grace.
Bless us and keep us close to your heart.
Amen.

Kate E. Ritger

To See Your Face

It is a most exciting thought,
That the struggle to remain focused,
On You, Father,
Is a temporary state of affairs.

It's so easy for me,
To always be pushing to remain
        under Your mantle,
So familiar am I to the running of this race,
That I sometimes forget
        that there is a finish line.

It is not because I am not aware
Of my future meeting with mortal death,
For I am aware of my death nearly everyday.

It is more because I view the next sixty years
As a struggle to keep You first in my life,
While still undertaking all the tasks
That this temporary state requires.

Help me to remember that the finish line—
Seeing Your face,
Will someday be Your gift to me.

William Degenhard

God, I have no defense.
I am lonely and miserable—
        for no real reason.
How can I spread your love
        when I don't have it?
How can I persuade others of your joy
when I am not joyful?
Why? How? What must I do?

Father, I'm tired. Please. Forgive me.
Father, forgive me
        because I fail to be sincere,
genuine, repentant, loving, selfless,
        trusting, committed.
I have questions
        that I love to pester myself with
until I can no longer smile.

Lord, turn my eyes to you.
        Let me be content
to live with my questions in your presence.
Enable me to love and to live in your joy.
Empty me Lord, and then consume me,
so that my actions are your actions.

To you, Lord, I pray. Amen.

Andrew Spidahl

Dear Lord, gracious Mother,
you have blessed me
        and showered me with love.
Sometimes do I demand a flood?
Am I not content with your shower?
Help me to love like you—I don't know
        if that is a practical request.
Help me to love and forgive
        and live my faith.
Amen.

Kate E. Ritger

Lectio

O God,
I make myself deaf
clamoring for your attention.

You wait for me
to listen
notice
open your Word
written on each moment of my life.

Jean Scoon

Lord,
To be brought to my knees in humiliation
only means that I no longer find
        any attraction in myself
—any intrinsic value, worth, power, ability,
        or merit.
What I find is that I need You.
I cannot exist apart from You or without You.
That I find my identity and power
through and in Your identity and power.
So that I know what Paul means
        when he says,
"When I am weak, then I am strong."
Amen.

Andrew Spidahl[30]

May the Blessing of God Rest upon Us—
Sufi Blessing

May the blessing of God rest upon us.
May God's peace abide in us.
May God's presence illuminate our hearts
Now and forevermore.[31]

I struggle, Father, to love you.
I know I love you, but I want to love you
the way I love the most important people
  in my life.
I want to love you
with the joy and passion and desire
  that I love others.
I will continue to seek you
  that I may love you better.
Amen.

Jennifer Wacek

May Jesus heal you, strengthen you,
  comfort you, and console you.
May He look upon you graciously
  and lovingly.
May He be compassionate toward you,
look kindly and mercifully and gently upon
  you.
May He give you His peace, joy,
  and happiness,
and may He bless you this day
  and every day.
Amen.

Marl Gapinski, O.S.B.

Notes

¹ Chittister, Joan. *The Rule of Benedict: Insights for the Ages* (New York: Crossroad, 1992) 19.

² Huub Oosterhuis, *Your Word Is Near: Contemporary Christian Prayers,* trans. N. D. Smith (New York: Newman Press, 1968) 10.

³ Submitted by Christian Breczinski. See *RB 1980: The Rule of St. Benedict,* ed. Timothy Fry, O.S.B., and others (Collegeville: Liturgical Press, 1981) ch. 18:1. The translation is that of *RB 1980,* not NRSV.

⁴ Submitted by Matthew Luft, O.S.B. This prayer is a translation of the Latin text found in *Calendarium et Proprium Missarum Totius Ordinis S.P.N. Benedicti,* novi eboraci, 1962; the Latin text is also found in the Benedictine Supplement of the Roman Missal (Benziger Brothers, 1962).

⁵ Submitted by Dunstan Moorse, O.S.B. Adapted for use in *Celebrating the Eucharist.*

⁶ Submitted by Nathan Hetrick. Copyright by Pax Christi U.S.A., W. 8th Street, Erie, Pa. 16502. Used with permission. Copies of "Prayer for World Peace" in 3" x 5" format can be purchased through the Pax Christi U.S.A. website, http://www.paxchristiusa.org (accessed April 1, 2004). "Vengeance is mine": in the *New American Bible,* see Romans 12:19 and the references there.

⁷ Submitted by Michael Kwatera, O.S.B.

⁸ Submitted by Verenice Ramler, O.S.B.

⁹ Submitted by Brian Reusch. "Song of Farewell" option used in the celebration of funerals.

¹⁰ Submitted by Rebecca Rawe. Copyright by The Institute of Jesuit Sources, St. Louis, Mo. Used with permission.

¹¹ Written by an adjunct instructor in the joint CSB/SJU Theology Department.

[12] Submitted by Verenice Ramler, O.S.B. Adapted from the Rite of Confirmation.

[13] Submitted by Matthew Luft, O.S.B.

[14] Submitted by Kate E. Ritger. *Interior Castle,* 2. From "A Cura di Batt," *Praying with Saint Teresa* (London: SPCK, 1988). Copyright by SPCK, Holy Trinity Church, 1 Marylebone Road, London, United Kingdom, NW1 4DU. Used with permission.

[15] Submitted by Diane Millis. This copyright material is taken from *A New Zealand Prayer Book—He Karakia Mihinare o Aotearoa* and is used with permission.

[16] Submitted by Nathan Hetrick.

[17] Submitted by Cyril Gorman, O.S.B. The English translation of the Universal Prayer from *The Roman Missal* © 1973, International Committee on English in the Liturgy, Inc. All rights reserved.

[18] Submitted by Ginny Clendenin. "Prayer for Healing" written by Msgr. James Moroney. Copyright 2003 by United States Conference of Catholic Bishops, Washington, D.C. All rights reserved. Reprinted with permission.

[19] Submitted by Nathan Hetrick. Inspired by the "Odes of Solomon," second century C.E. Copyright by GIA Publications, Inc., Chicago, Ill. All rights reserved. Used with permission.

[20] Submitted by Matthew Luft, O.S.B. The translation is that of *RB 1980,* except that "In" is "in," being in mid-sentence. NRSV translates this differently.

[21] Submitted by Matthew Luft, O.S.B.

[22] Submitted by Wilfred Theisen, O.S.B.

[23] Inspired by Thich Nhat Hanh's explanation of the 5 prostrations in *Present Moment, Precious Moment,* retreat on tape.

[24] Submitted by Katherine Kraft, O.S.B. *Poems,* 9. From "A Cura di Batt," *Praying with Saint Teresa* (London: SPCK, 1988). Copyright by SPCK, Holy Trinity Church, 1 Marylebone Road, London, United Kingdom, NW1 4DU. Used with permission.

[25] The last line of "Faithfulness" inspired by Abbot Timothy Kelly's remark: "The essence of God's love is faithfulness."

[26] Submitted by Ginny Clendenin.

[27] Submitted by Joe Sacksteder.

[28] Submitted by Nathan Hetrick. Copyright by GIA Publications, Inc., Chicago, Ill. All rights reserved. Used with permission.

[29] Submitted by Kate E. Ritger. *The Way of Perfection*, 26. From "A Cura di Batt," *Praying with Saint Teresa* (London: SPCK, 1988). Copyright by SPCK, Holy Trinity Church, 1 Marylebone Road, London, United Kingdom, NW1 4DU. Used with permission.

[30] 2 Cor 12:10: "when I am weak, then I am strong" (NAB).

[31] Submitted by Nathan Hetrick. Copyright by GIA Publications, Inc., Chicago, Ill. All rights reserved. Used with permission.

Photographs on pp. x, 20, 58, and 120 are from the Liturgical Press Archives.

Photograph on p. 36 taken and submitted by Peter Ehresmann.

Photographs on pp. 84 and 104 courtesy of Joachim Rhoades, O.S.B.